THIS BOOK BELONGS TO:

_____

Tigers are wild beasts with great might...

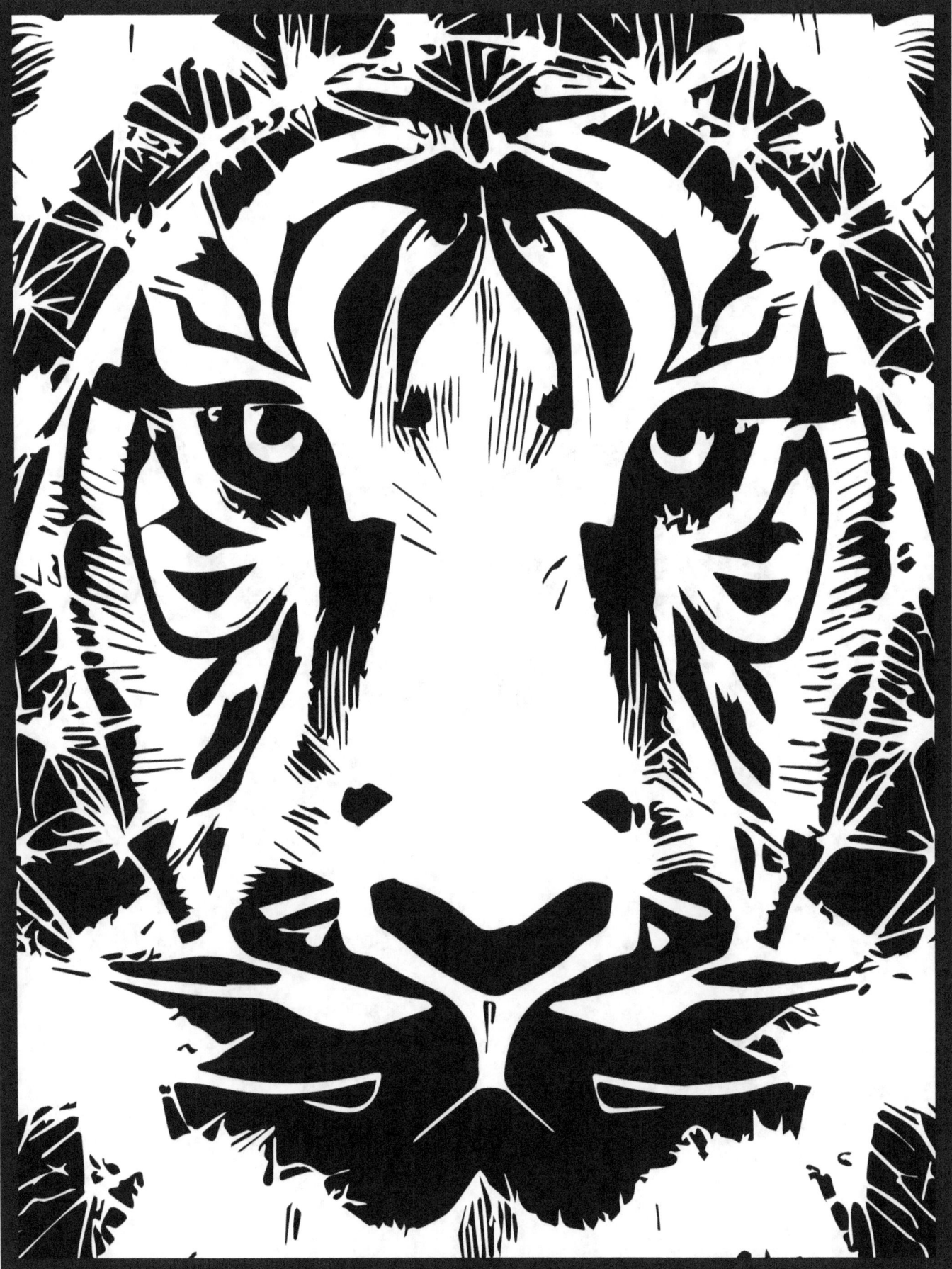

Six subspecies in existence, what a sight

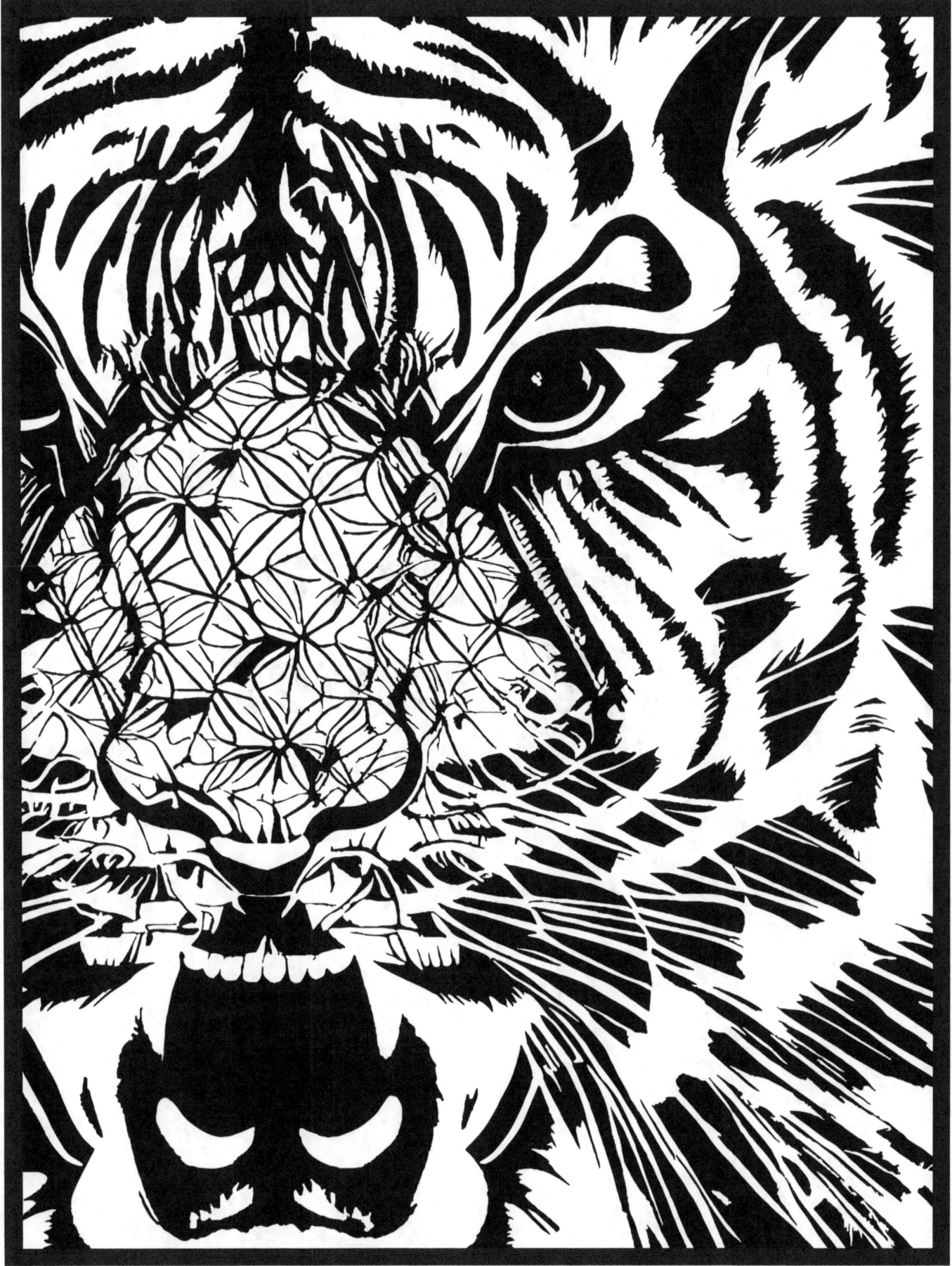

They weigh quite a lot, up to 600 pounds

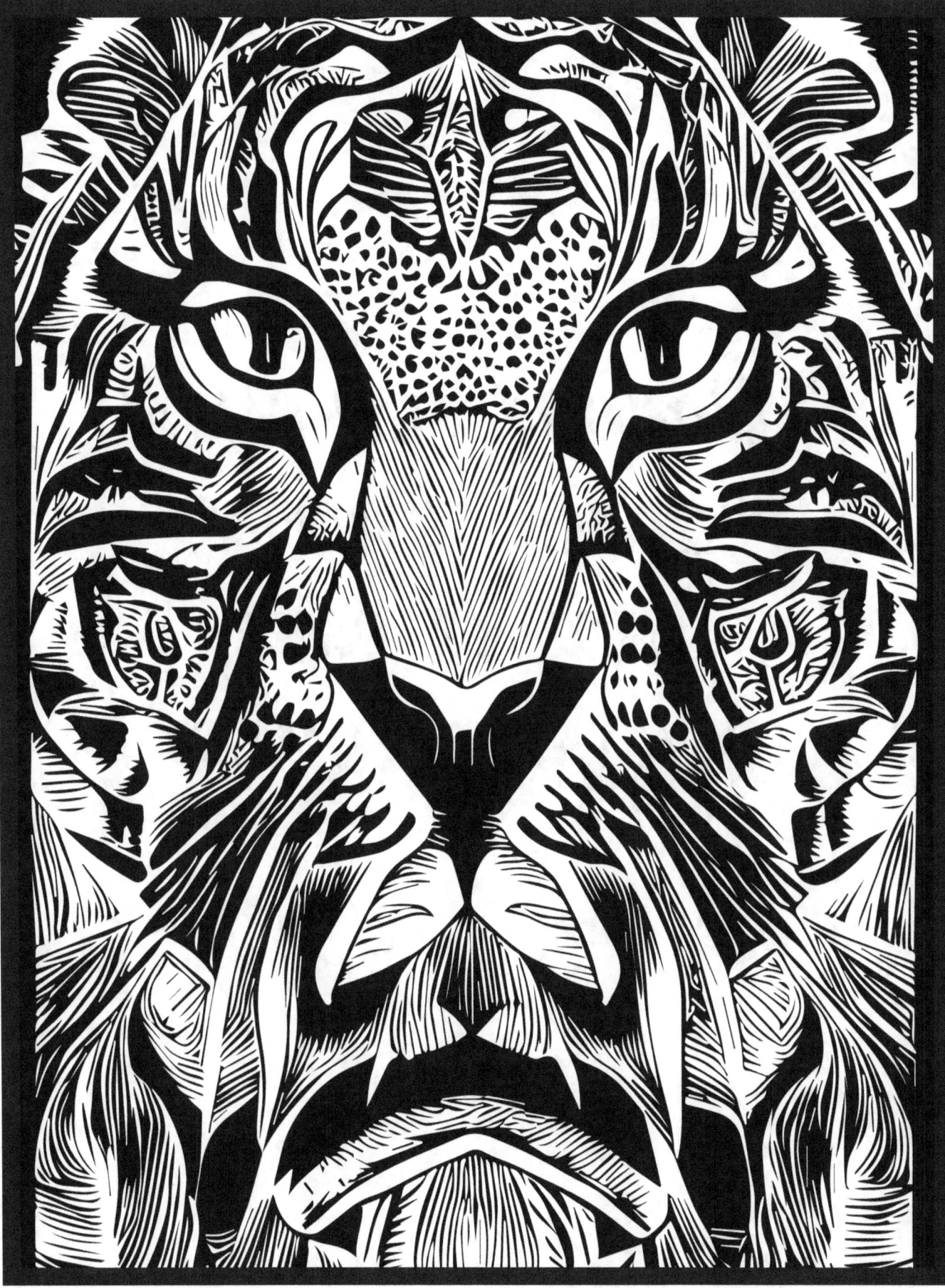

Orange fur with black stripes, stalks prey without sounds

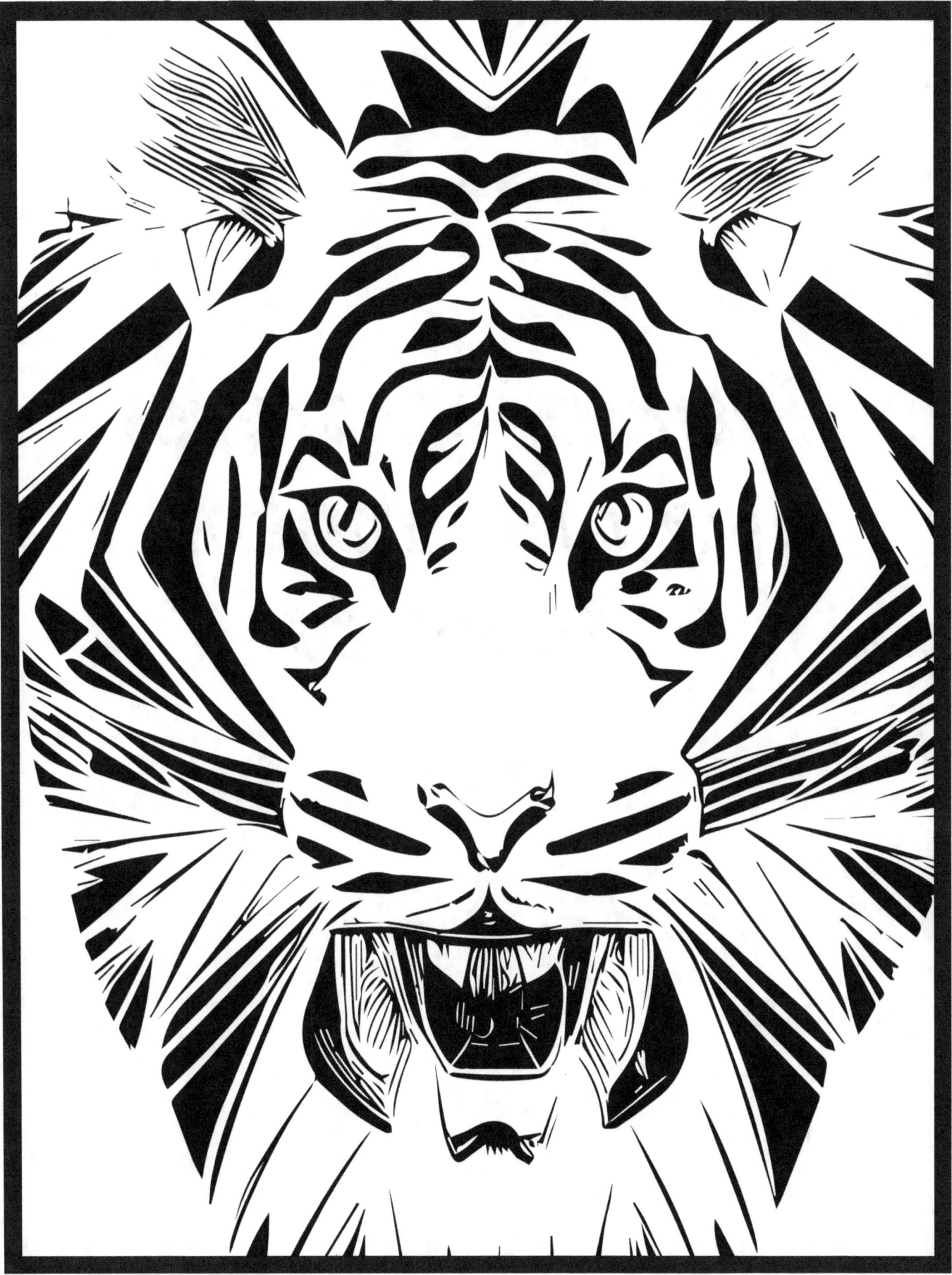

Solitary creatures, only come together to breed

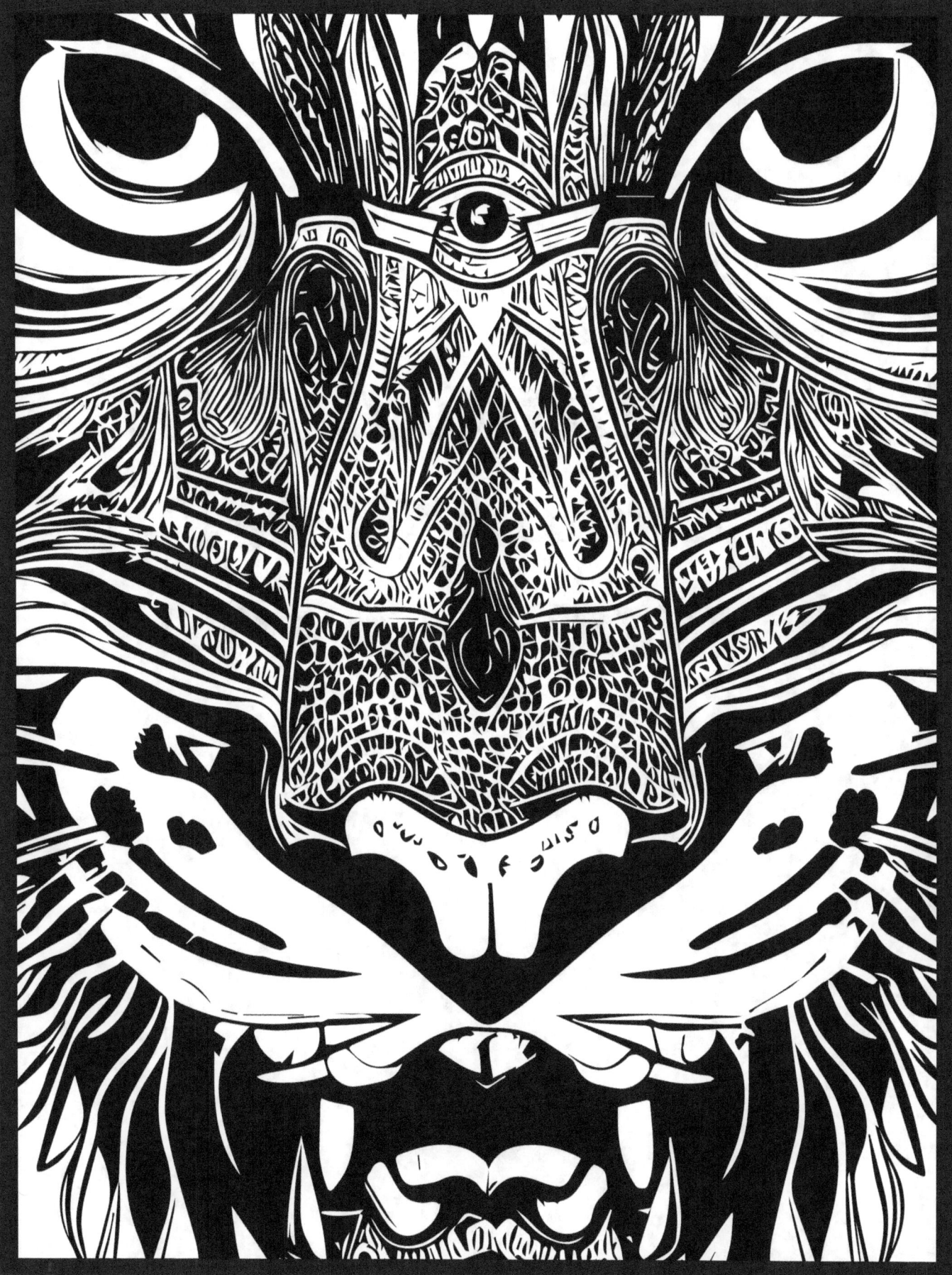

Carnivorous diet, ungulates are their main feed

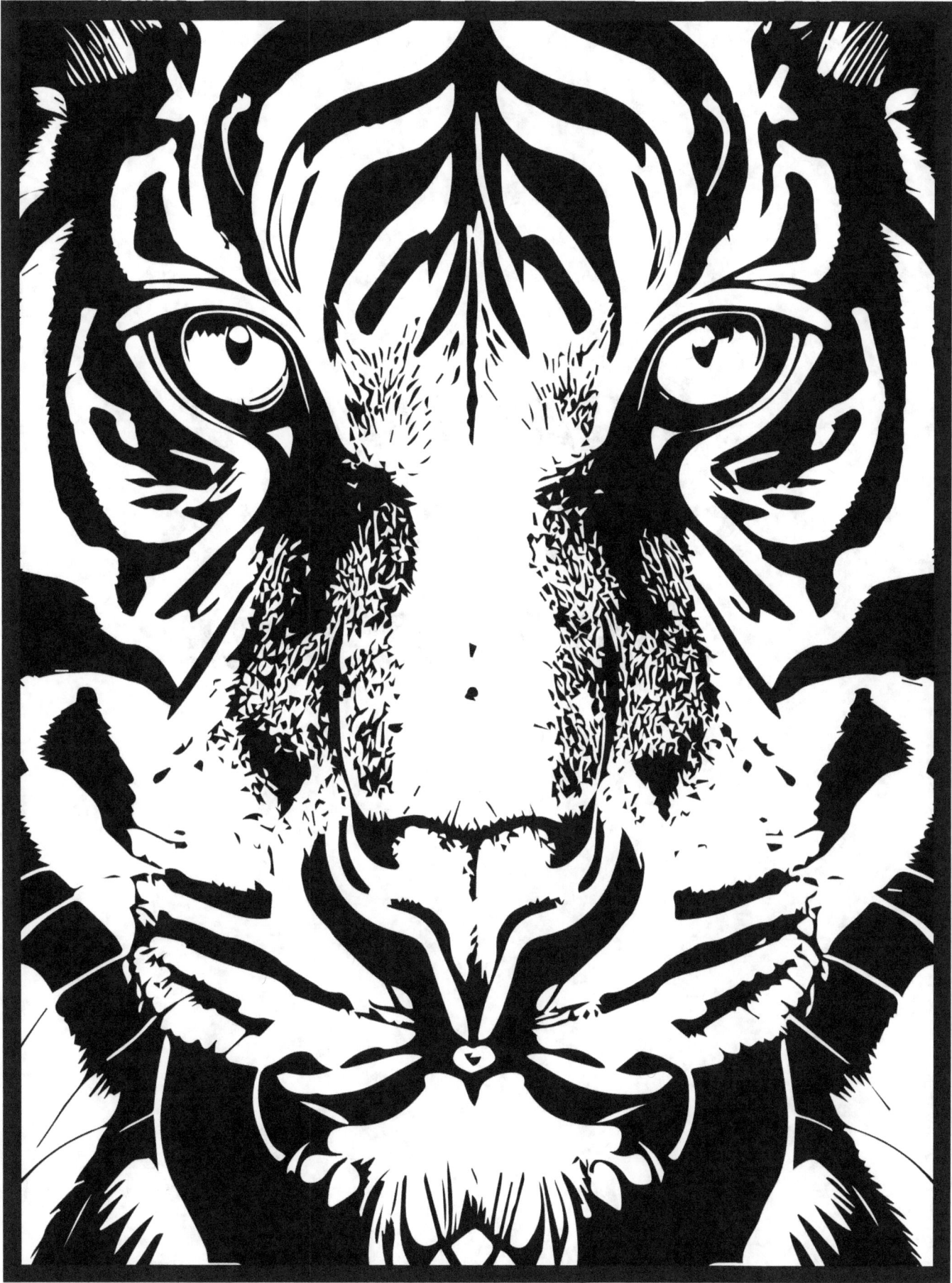

Tigers love to swim, for miles they"ll paddle

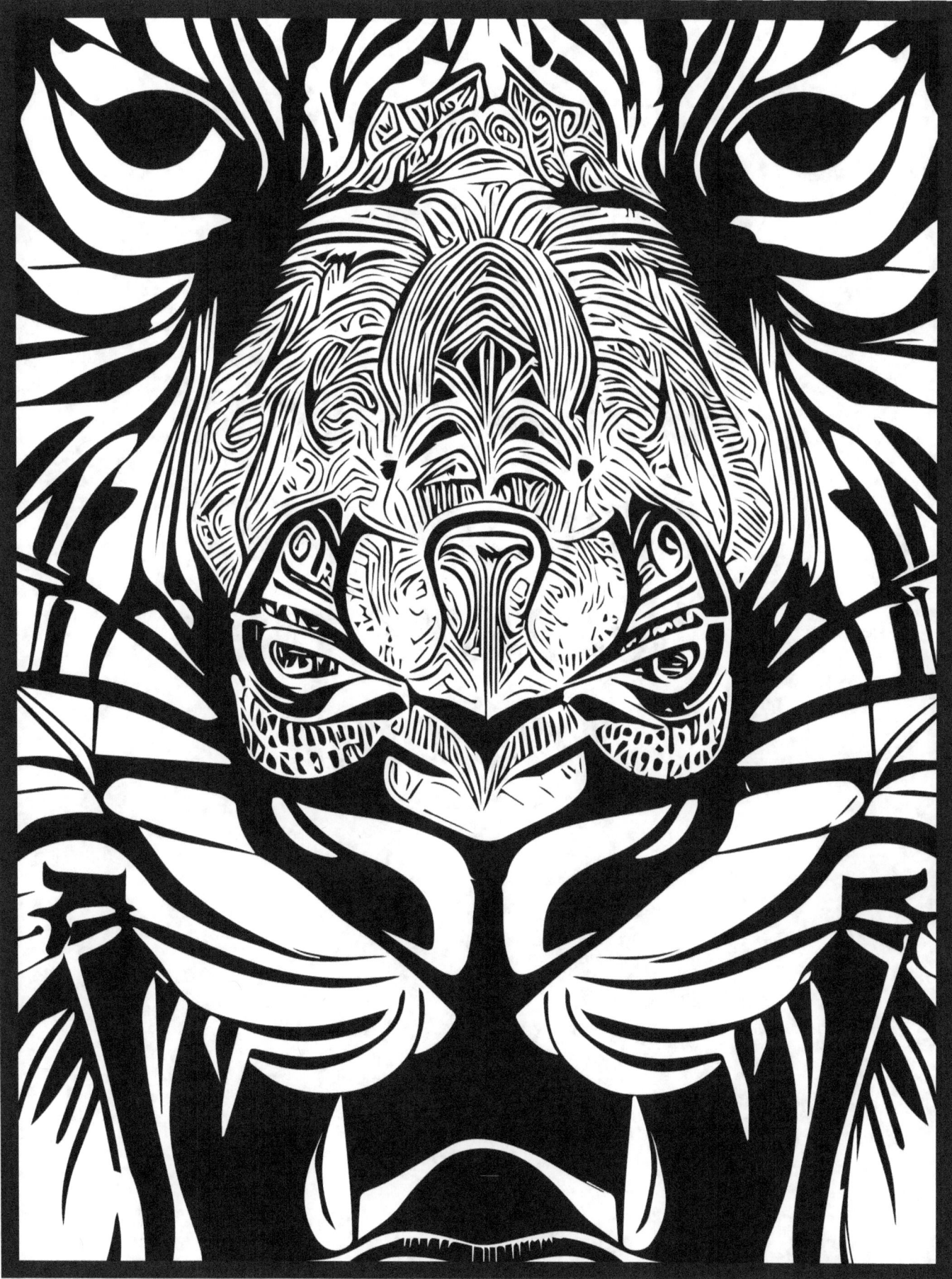

In Asia they're from, in many countries they straddle

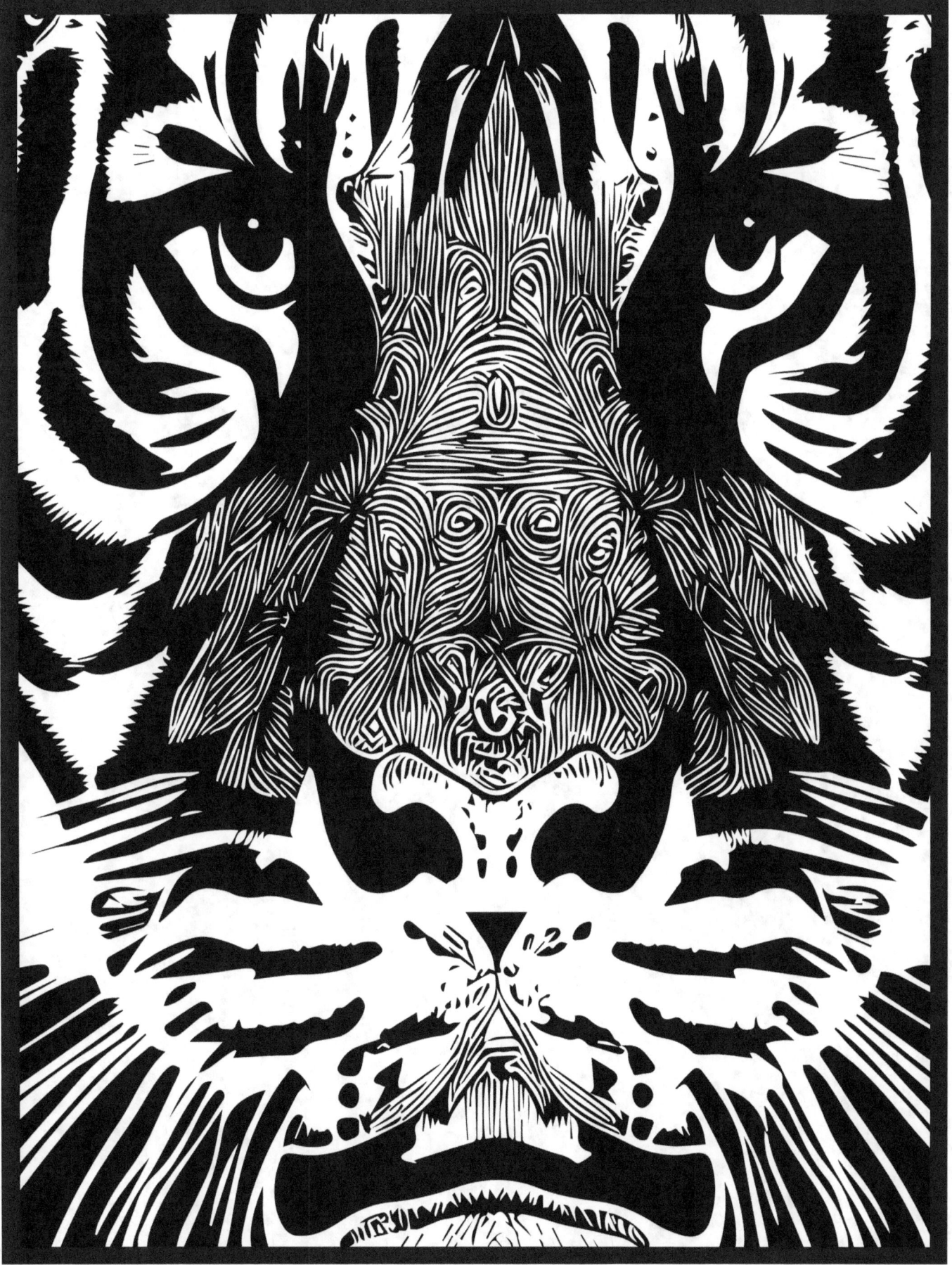

Apex predators, none can bring them down

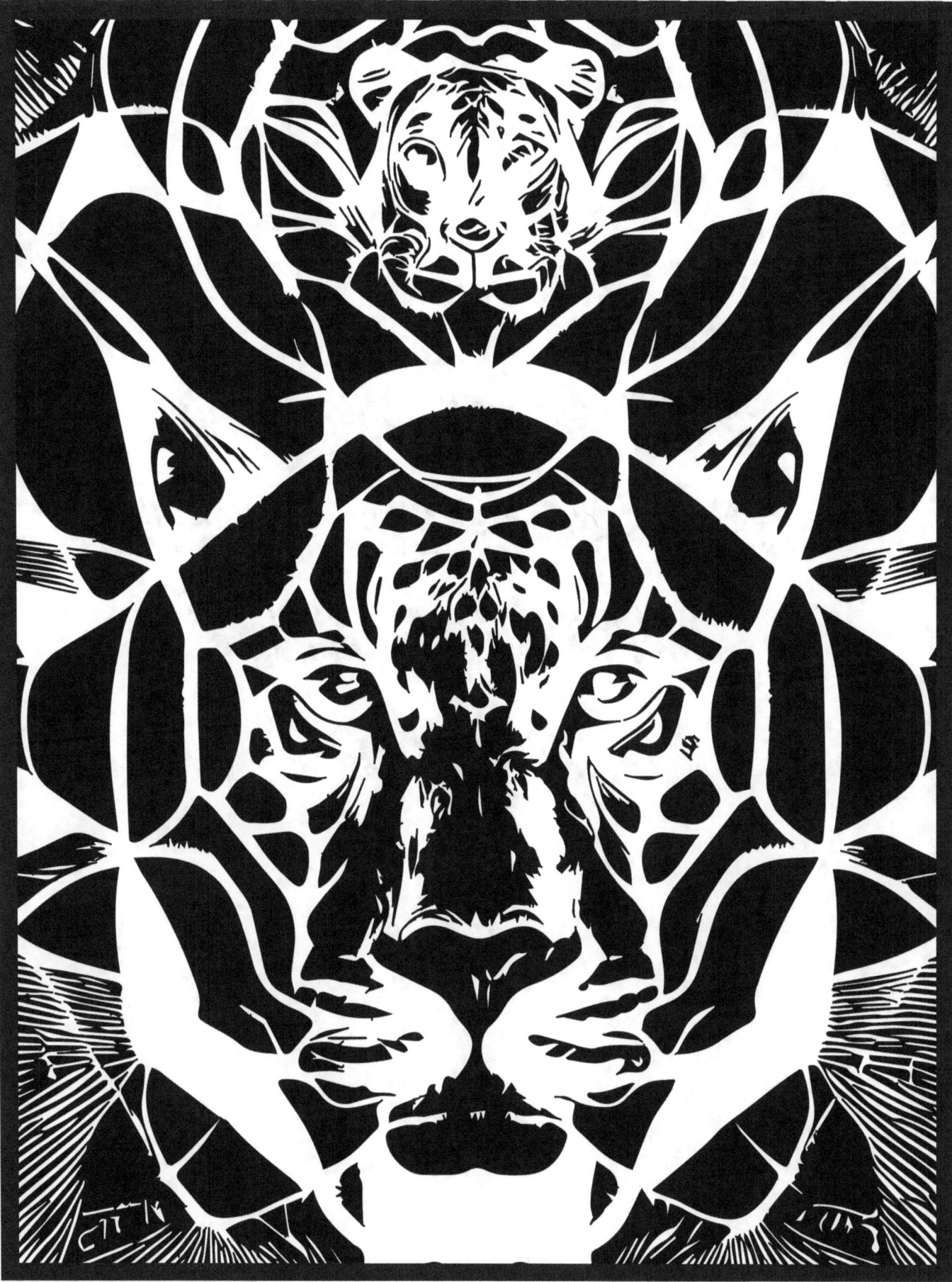

But now they're endangered, their numbers have drown

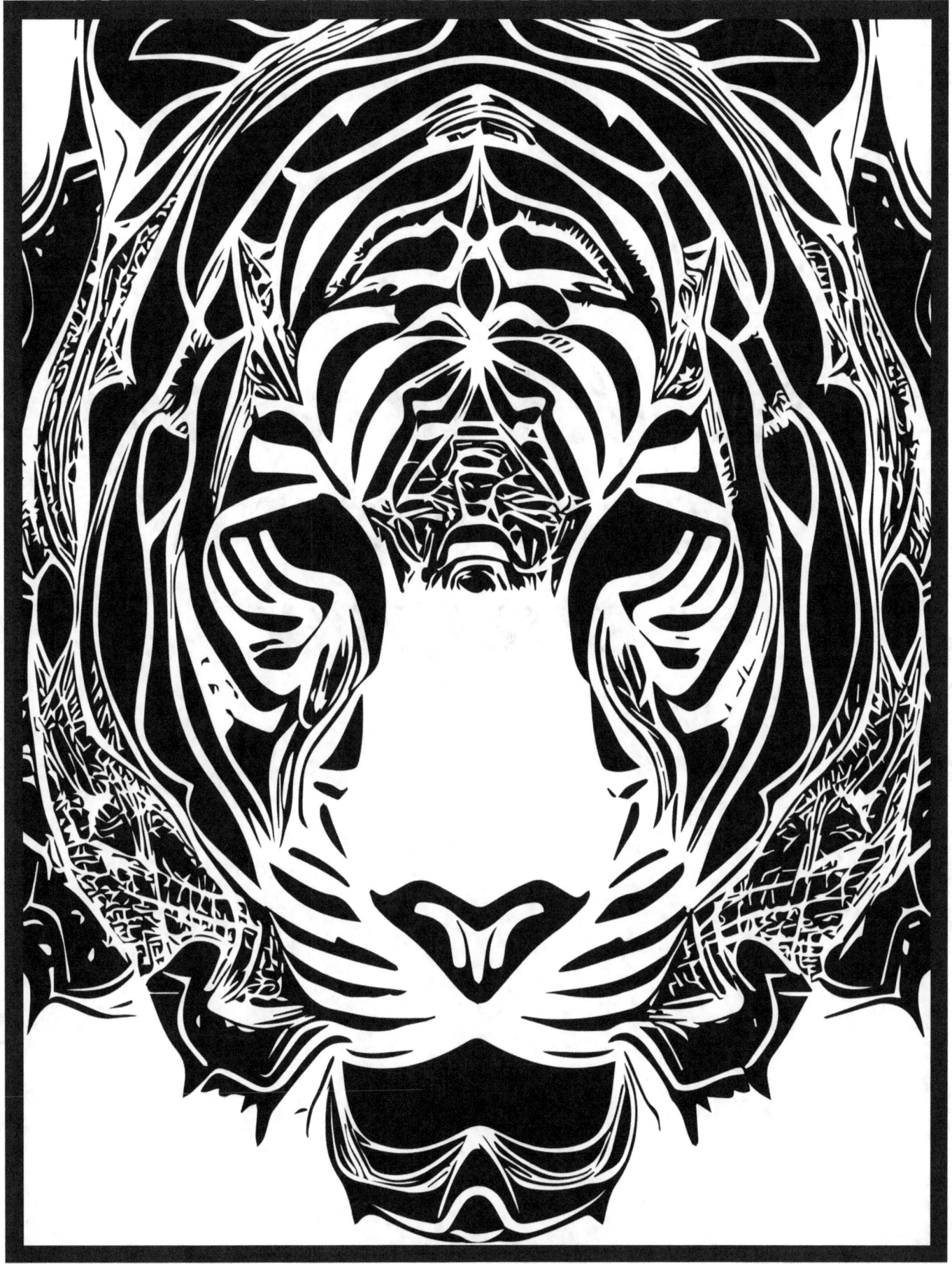

The IUCN lists them as, in danger of extinction

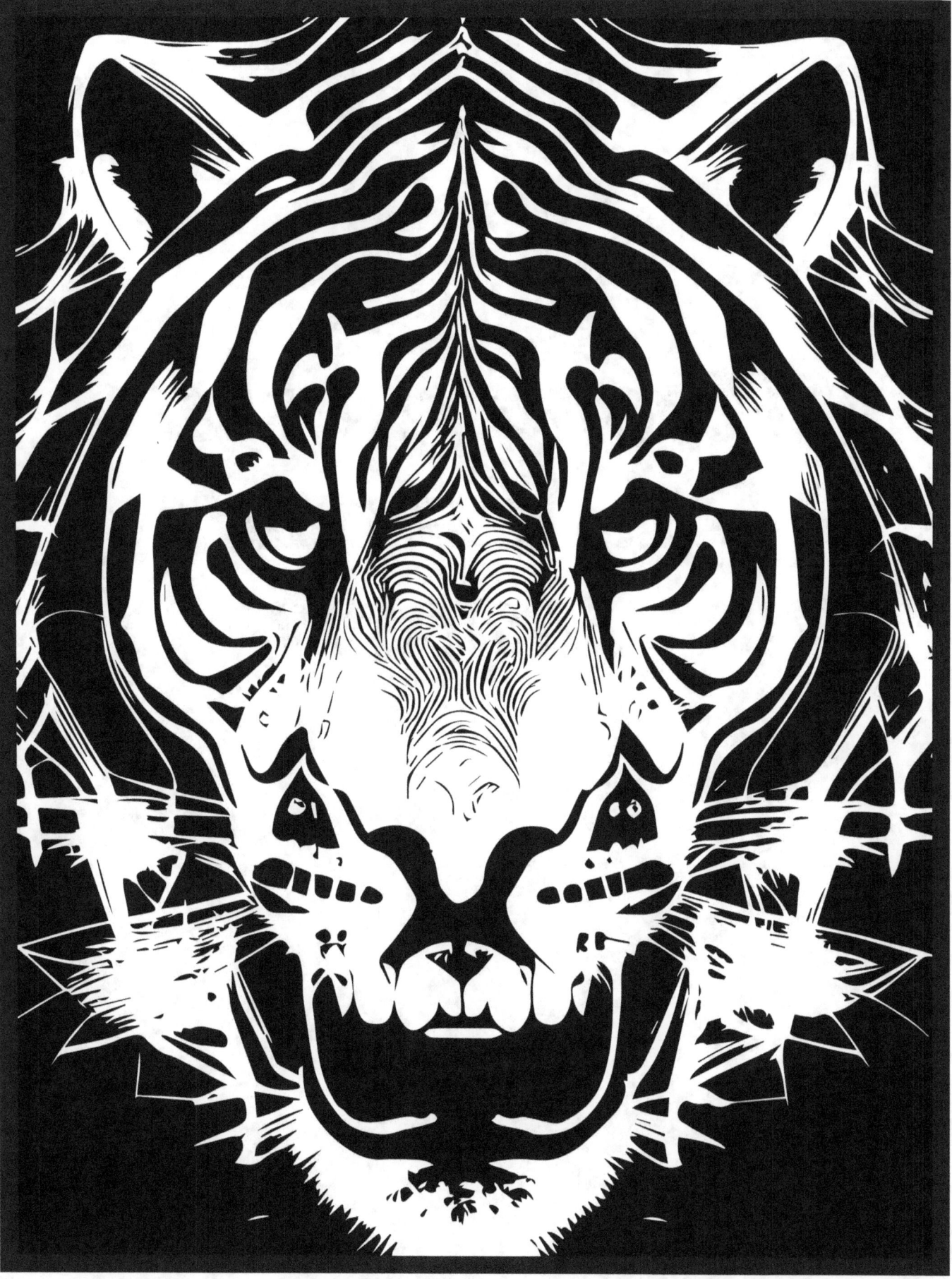

Poached for their fur, a terrible addiction

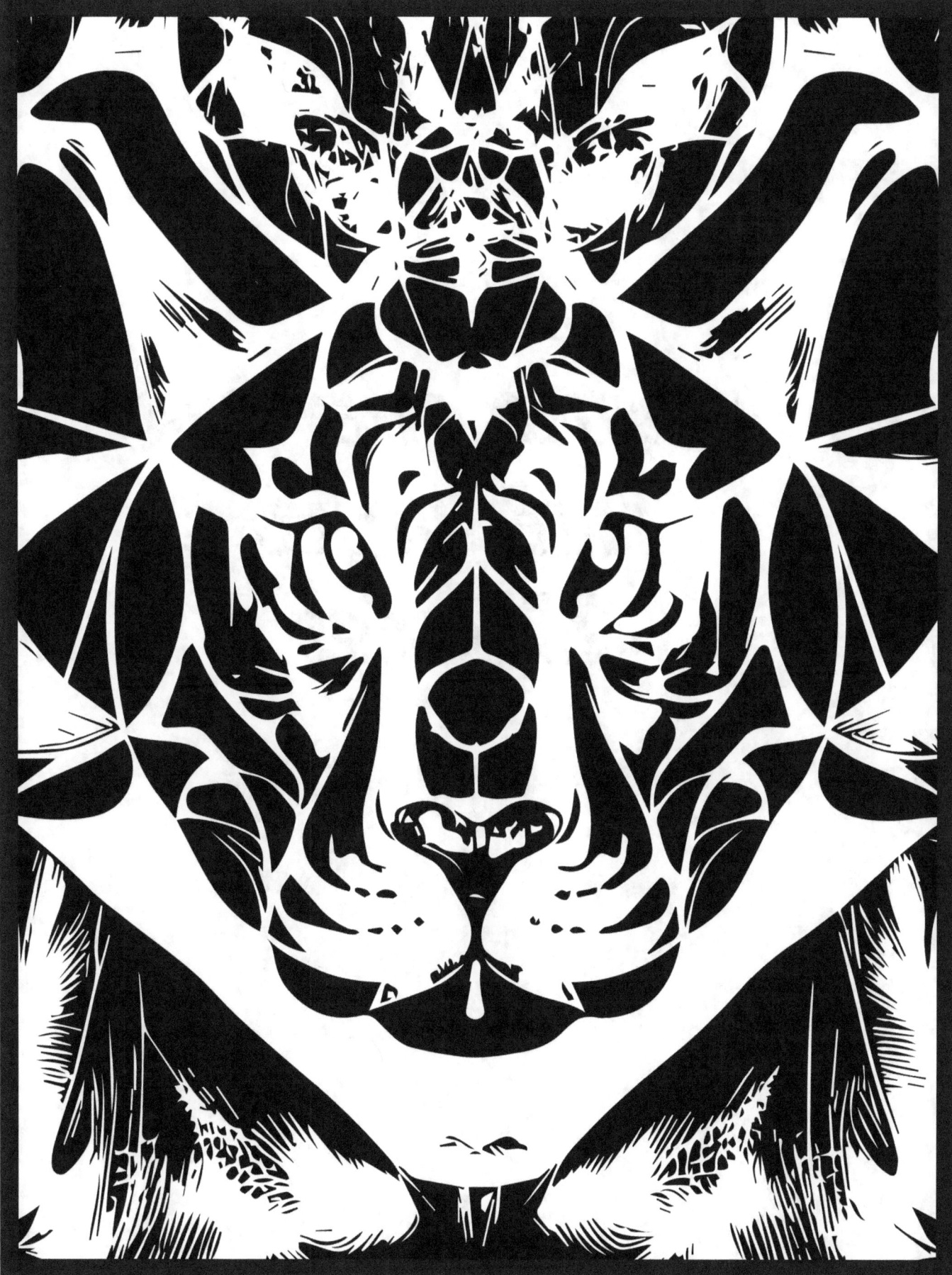

In wild they can live, up to 25 years

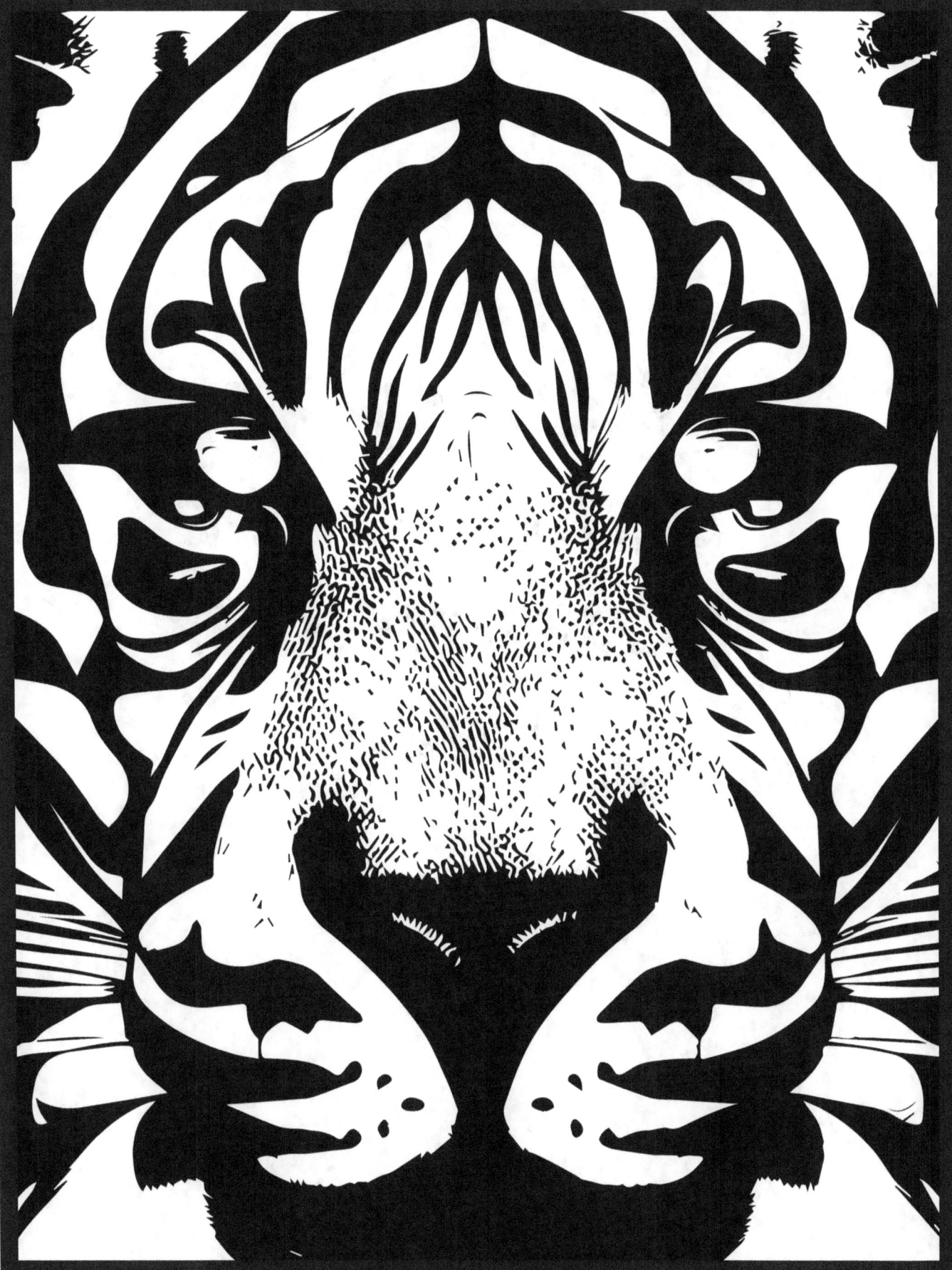

Maintaining balance, their ecosystem they steer

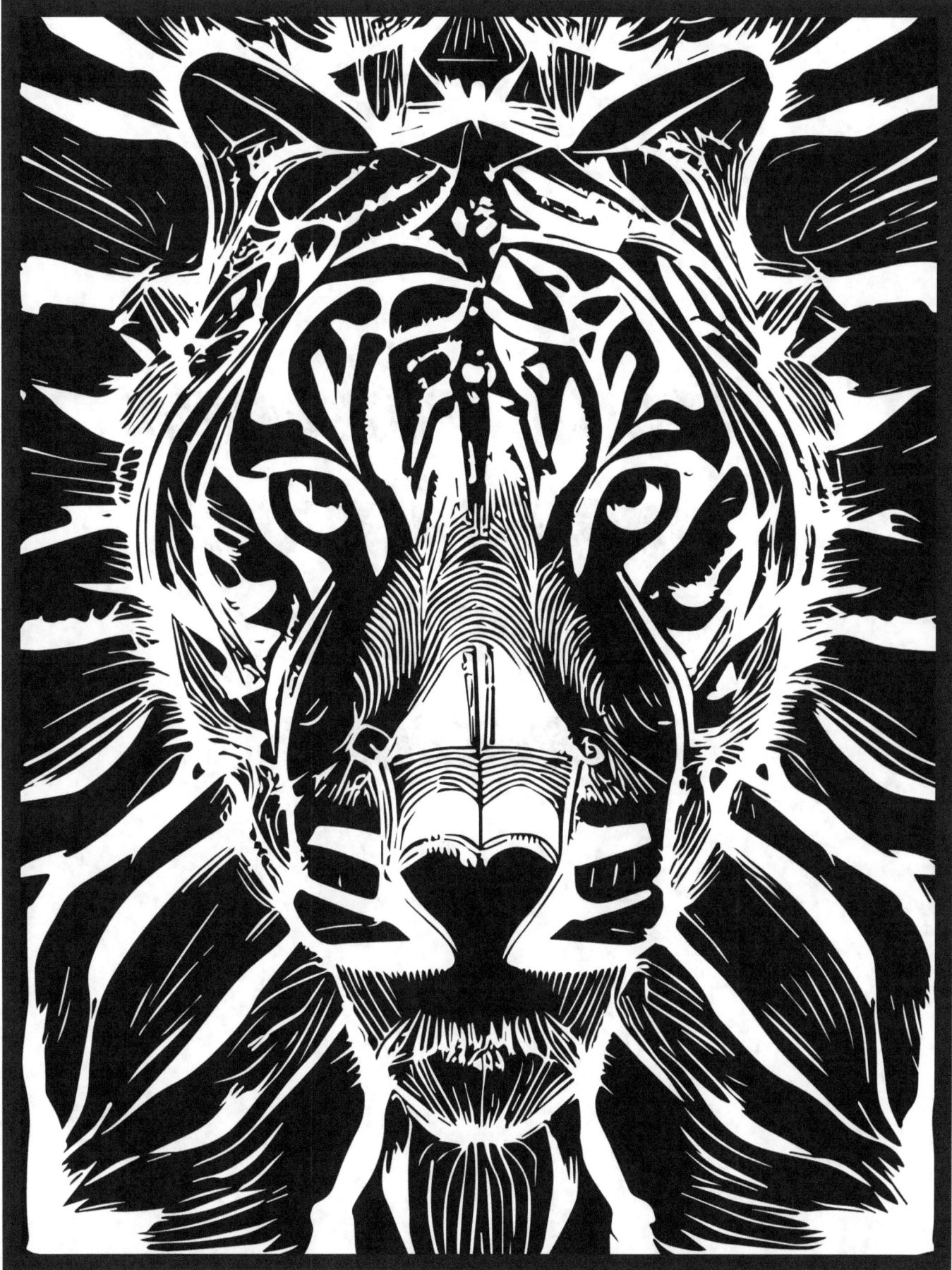

Strong, powerful and graceful, tigers are a treasure

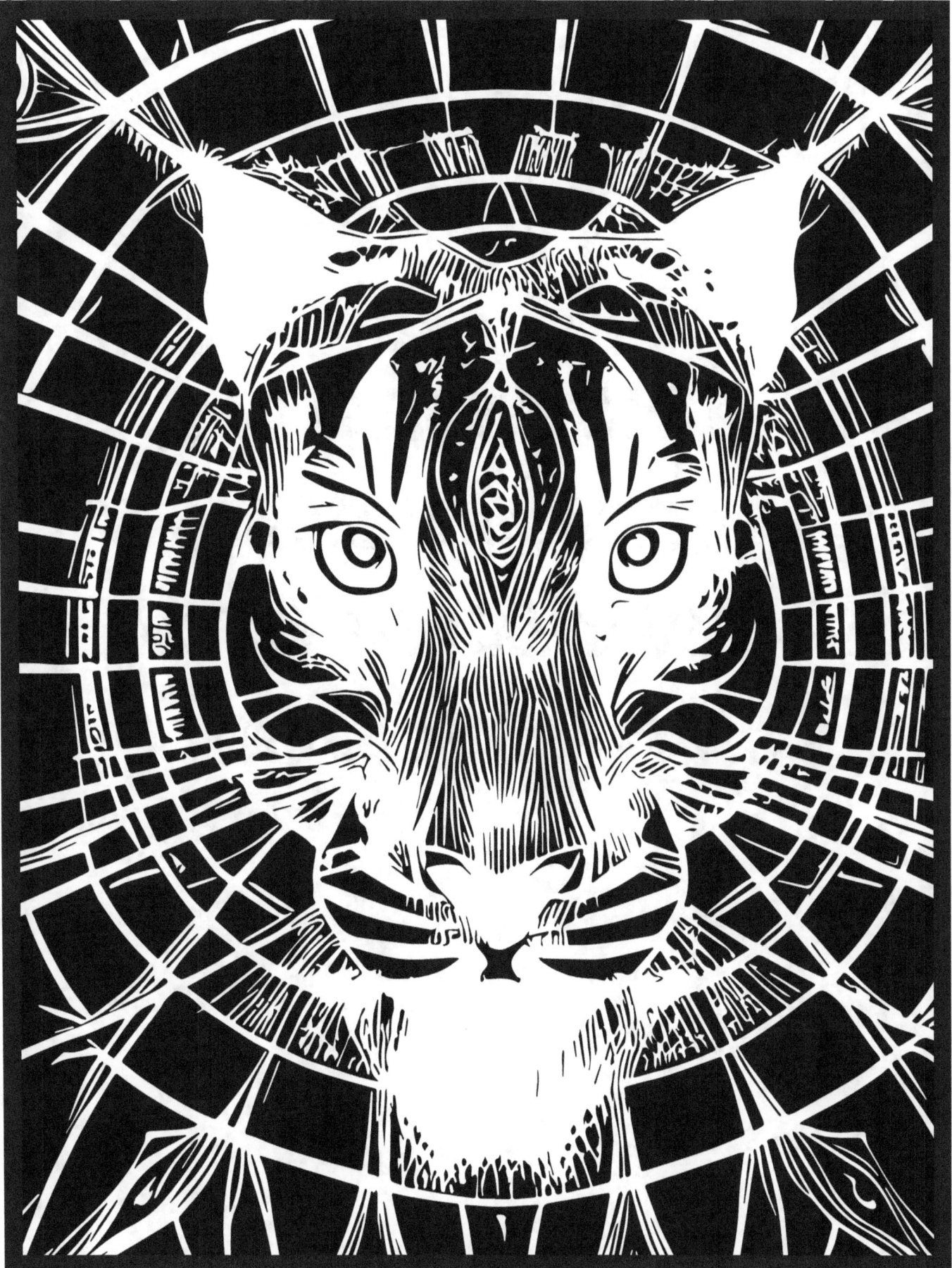

APEX PREDATORS, NONE CAN BRING THEM DOWN WITH WHATSOEVER

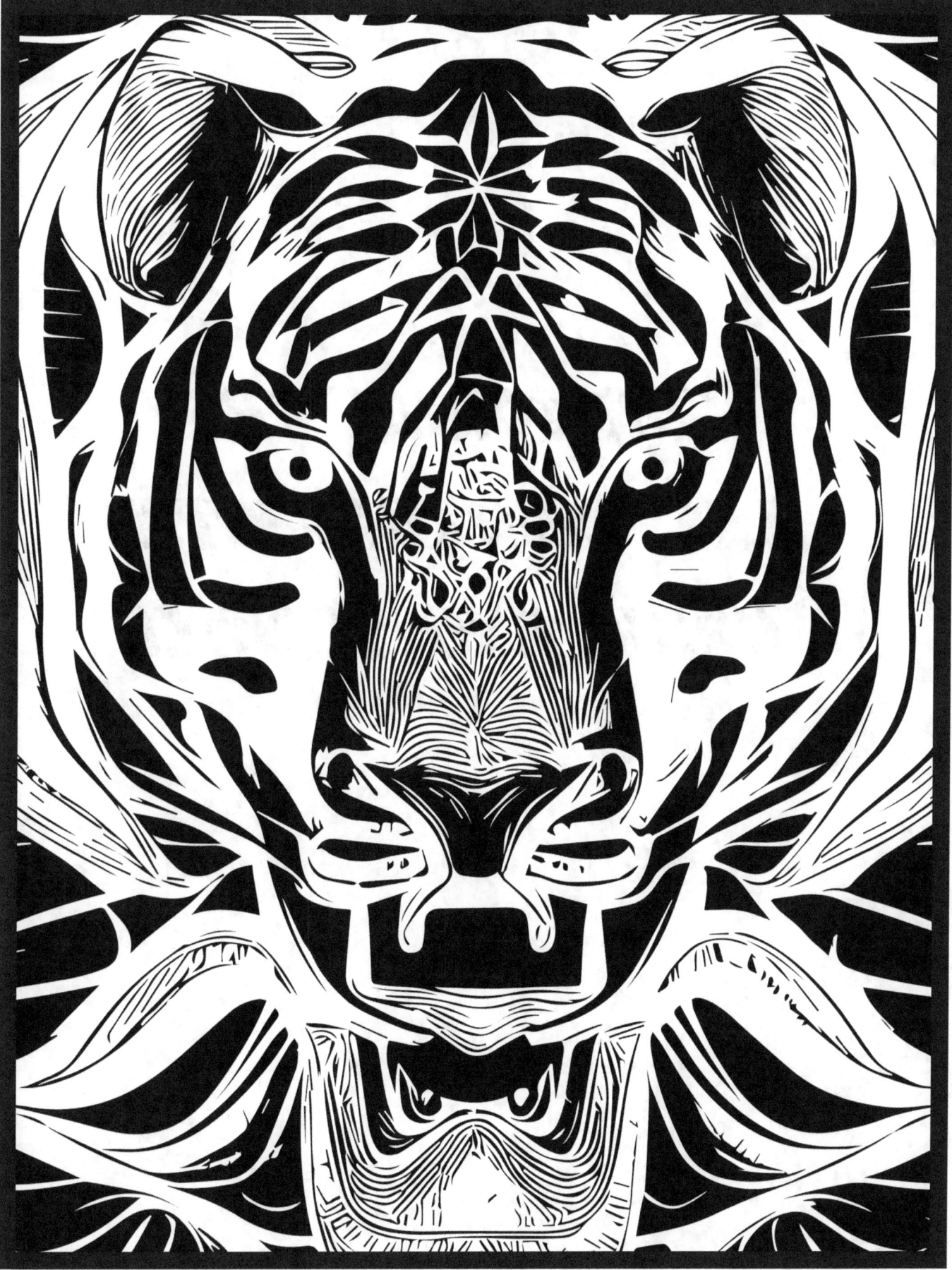

Territorial they are, marking with urine and scratch

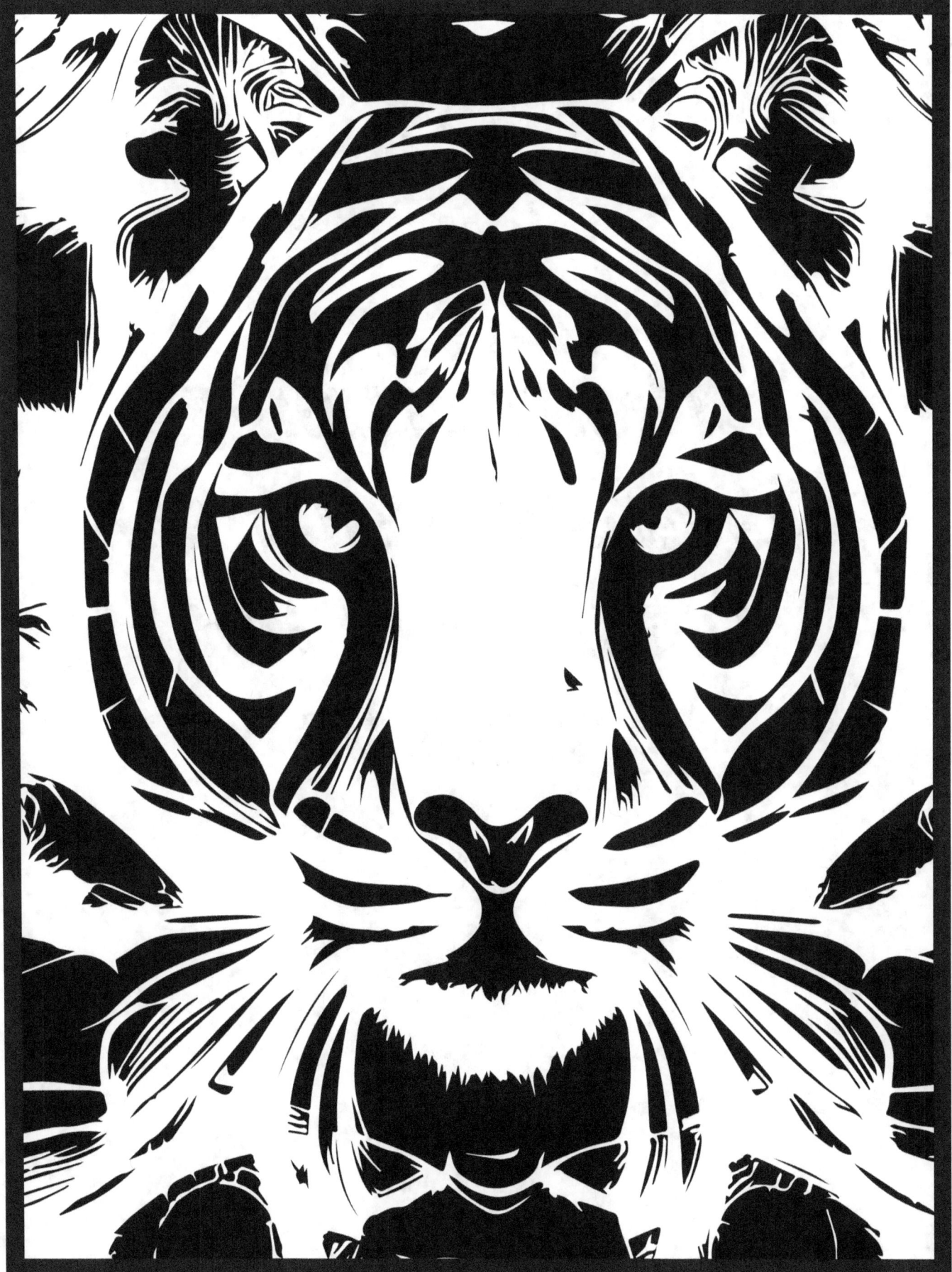

Night vision's excellent, they can see 6 times more than us

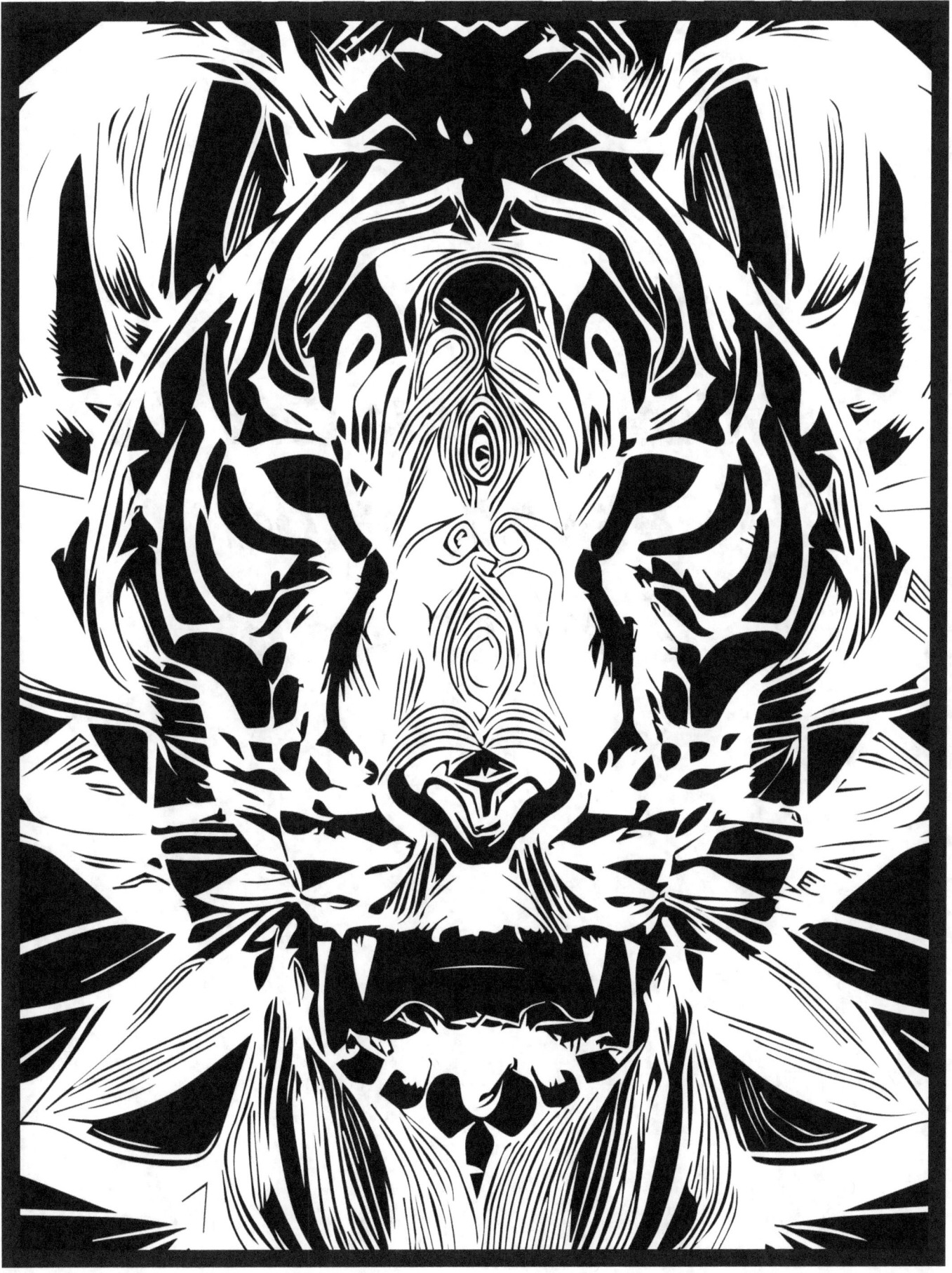

Tigers roar can be heard, from 2 miles away

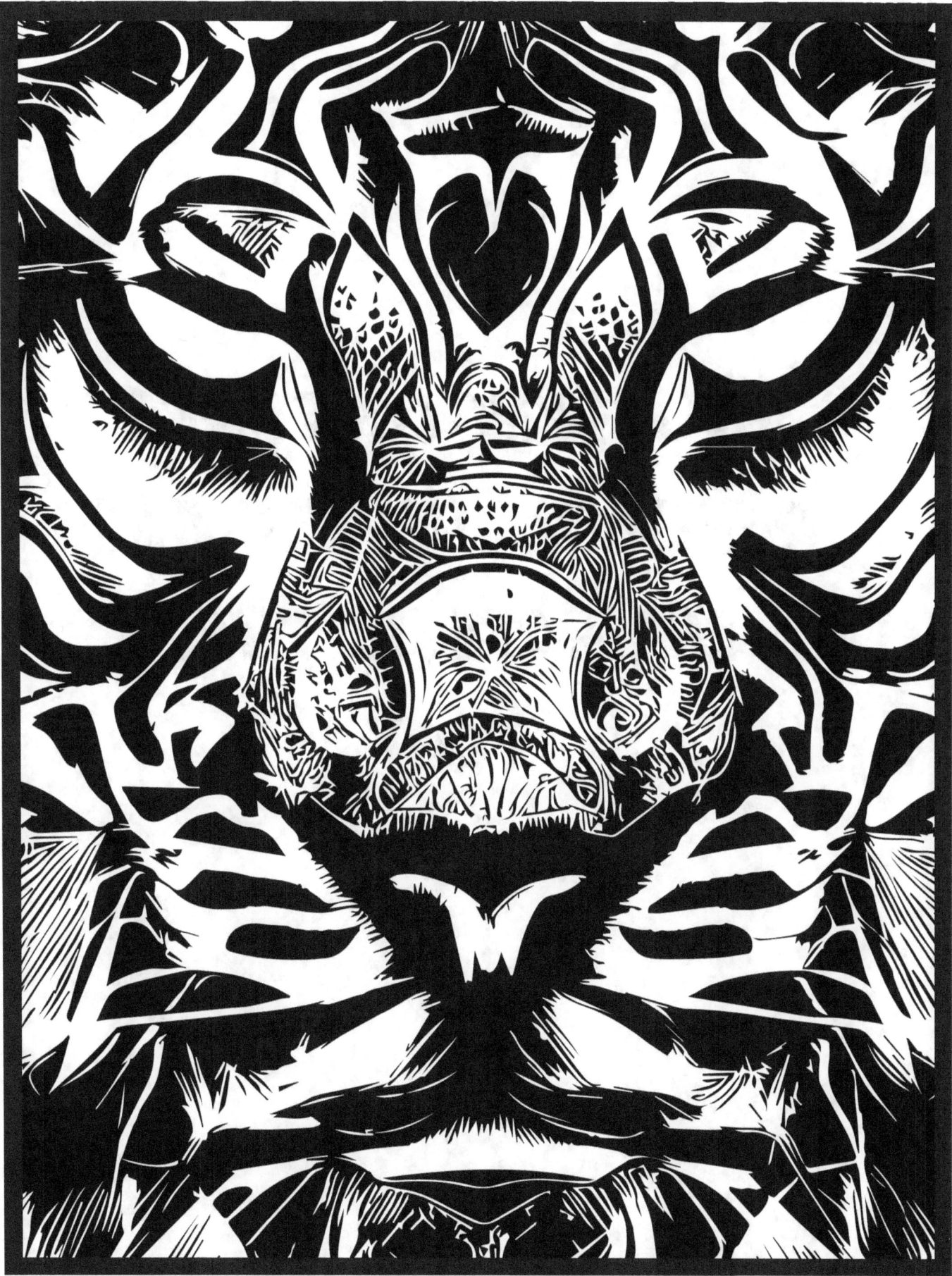

In Asian cultures revered, in art and literature they play

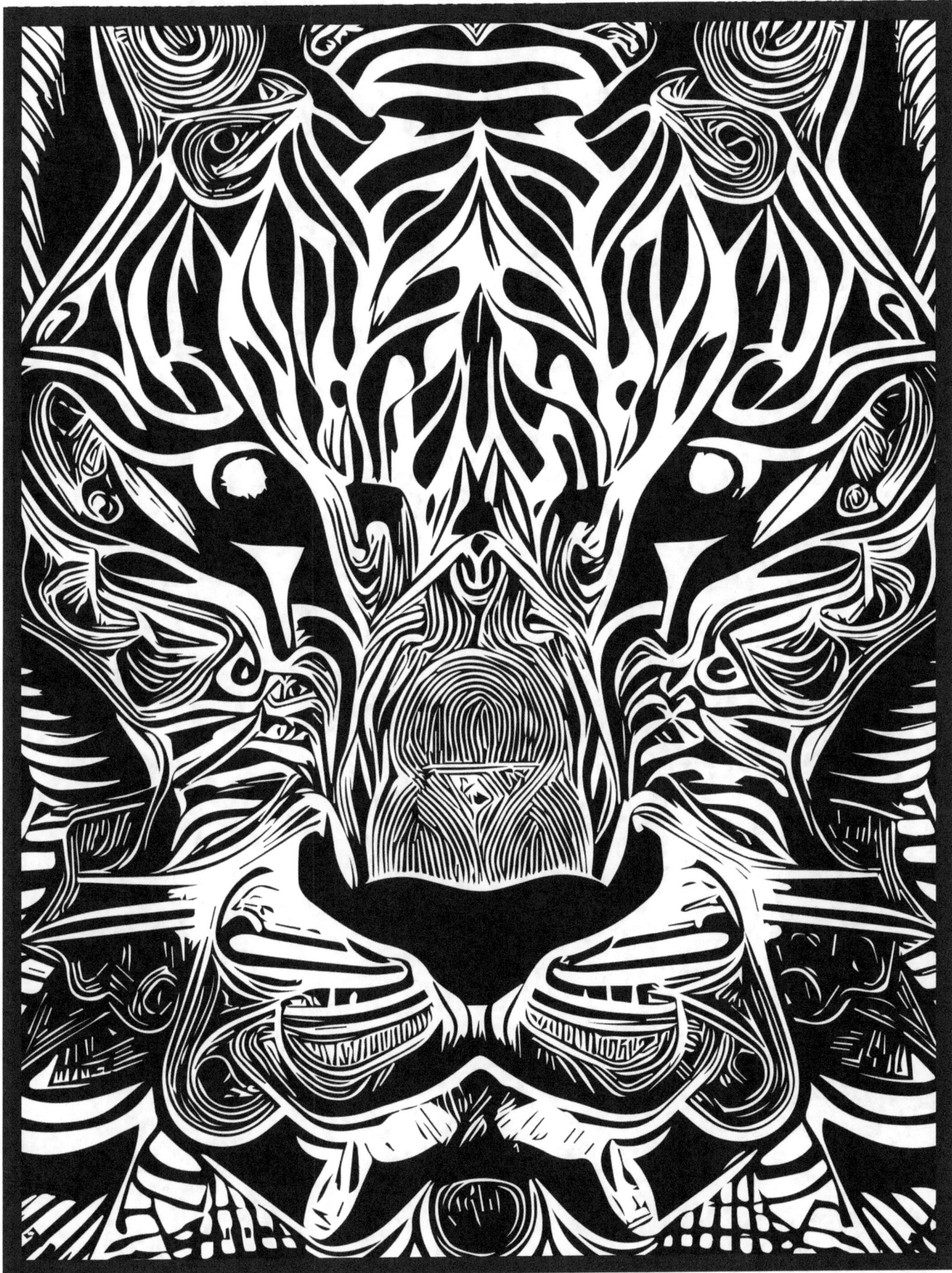

www.ingramcontent.com/pod-product-compliance
Lightning Source LLC
Chambersburg PA
CBHW081100240526
45465CB00025B/2776